Vintage Black

Andrea Johnson Books Publishing

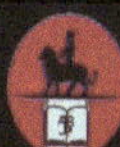

Vintage Black

© 2021 Sefa Noir. All rights reserved.

Cover art designed by Andrea Johnson Books Publishing

No part of this book may be reproduced, stored in a retrieval system, or transmitted by any means without the written permission of the author.

First published by Andrea Johnson Books Publishing. 05/07/2021

6565 N. MacArthur Blvd, Suite 225 Dallas, TX. 75039 www.Ajbpublishing.com

This book is a work of fiction. Names, characters, places, and incidents are the product of the author's imagination or are used fictitiously. Any resemblance to actual events, locales, or persons, living or dead, is coincidental.

Because of the dynamic nature of the Internet, any web addresses or links contained in this book may have changed since publication and may no longer be valid. The views expressed in this work are solely those of the author and do not necessarily reflect the views of the publisher, and the publisher herby disclaims any responsibility for them.

ISBN: 978-0-578-86803-5

Vintage Black

SEFA NOIR

For Beautiful Black Lovers Everywhere

Kawo! Kabiosile Sango

Table of Contents

There You Were

And there you were, unlike the multitudes you cared little about the public show.

You thought you were hiding in your simple quiet existence, but I heard you.

My soul and spirit heard you as if to say we were reunited from a time long ago.

In your presence, I stood taller and straighter, my chest broadened, my nose flared like A peacock's mating… you were to be mine and I knew it even if you didn't.

And there you were with eyes like history, and lips sweeter than any fairy tale.

I longed to be with you, to smell you, to taste you to touch you, but not like the others.

I wanted to ignite that forbidden passion within you, I wanted and desperately needed the rawness of your lust – modern day politeness and etiquette had no use in our forever.

You are everything and nothing that I have craved and prayed for, and in a moment's blink,

You stood before me on a street corner and I had no words to give you,

only the impatient beating of my heart in my chest could be heard. And there you were, and I knew that my life would never be the same.

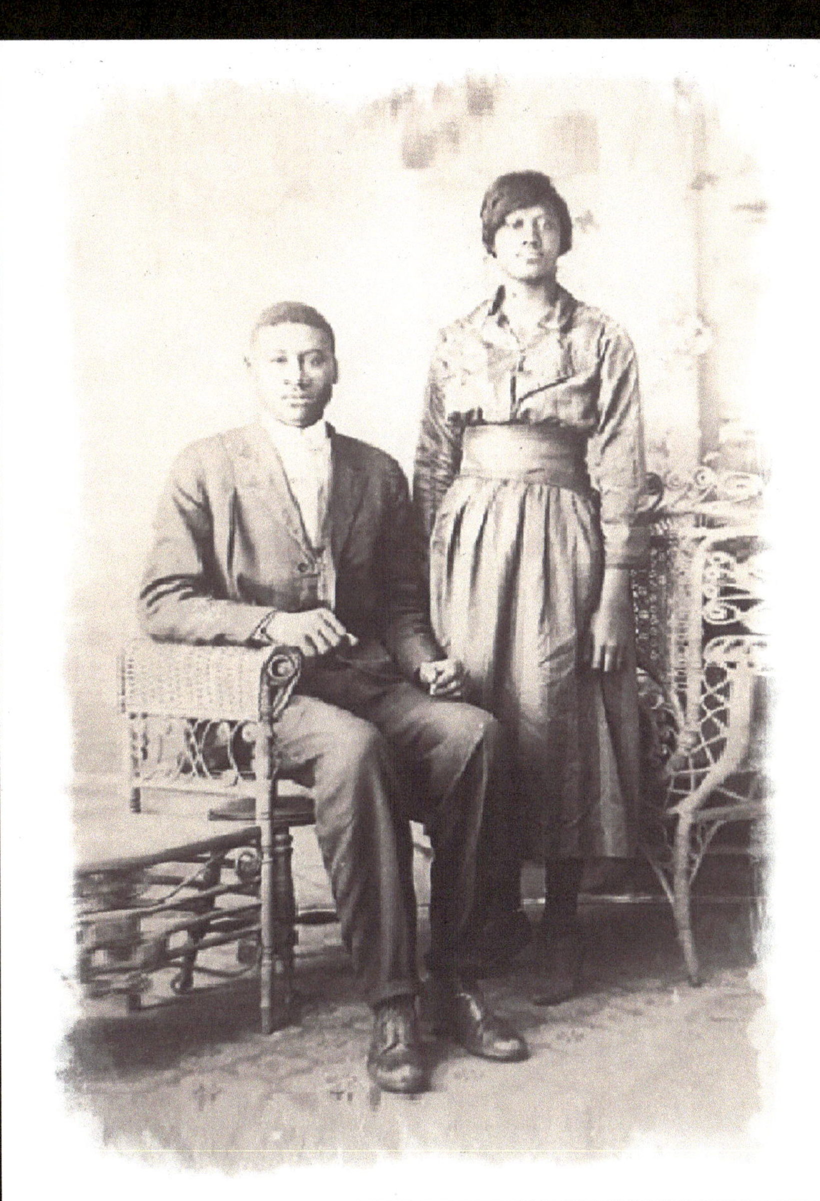

The Longing

I long to be in your presence simply and concretely lying together with my heart pressed tightly against your back…me supporting you and you protecting me.

I long to know your thoughts, complex and deep–so that your visions may give me wings to soar again. I long to taste your kiss, sweet and passionate with a purposeful intensity – in that moment you became my King.

I lie here in my bed and I feel the magnetic pull of your soul…. It creates this need within me to constantly write to you, for you, and about you as if the universe has chosen me to be your divine messenger. I see and feel your greatness and I am enraptured by the depth and beauty that is your blackness. I exhale my truth and you use it like a sail for your boat to reach our destiny.

I long to be with you always.

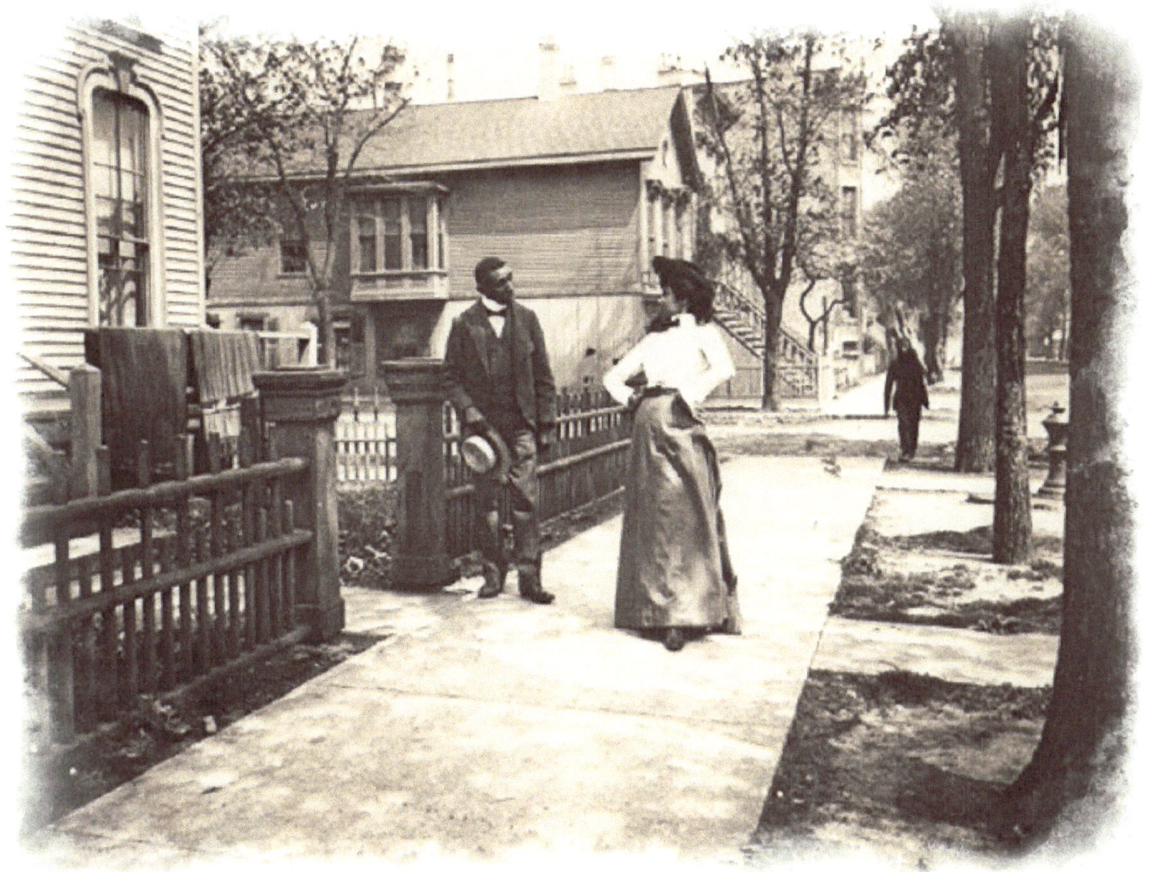

If Need Be

We have been each other's safe harbor. We have weathered the storms, and arrows of the wars waged against our people. We had nothing but each other and for some, even that was too much.

We tended to each other's aches and pains and found ecstasy in our simple cabin by the fire.

When you looked at me across the cotton field, I heard every word your heart said, and I pushed on.

I refused to give up no matter what they did to us – I wouldn't allow them to separate us, and if they could, I promise I would find my way back to you over and over again.

I had no fear then because I had you ... now that time has passed, and the wrinkles tell the story on my face, I am terrified. I plead each night for father death not to take you from me in the night. We have stood the test of time and now time is chasing our love. I will not give in to its demands. We belong together even in death if need be – I will gladly take the Baron's other hand and walk with you into the essence. I cannot, I will not be without you.

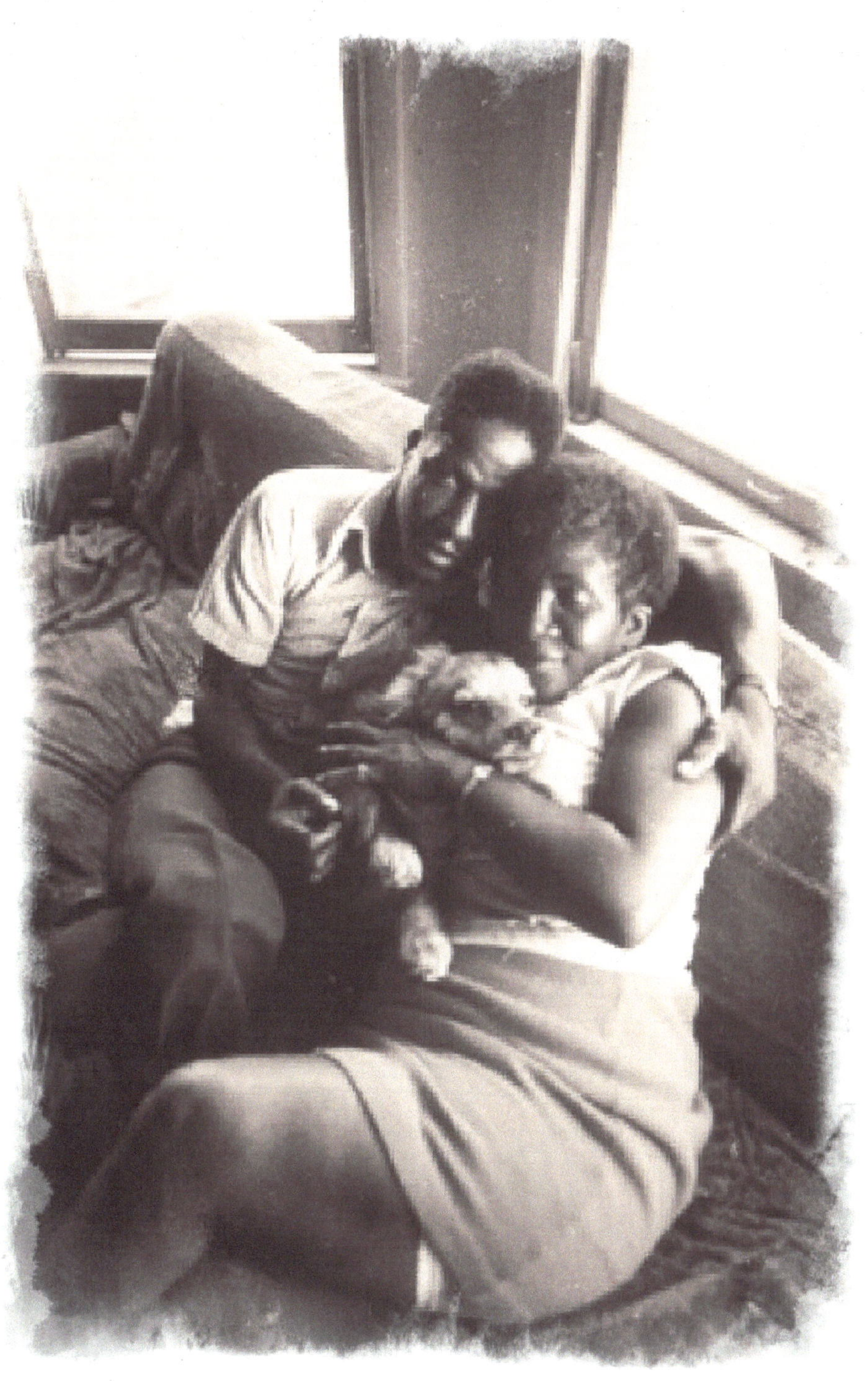

Lost and Found

How did we find each other? They set us free with no history and no name to claim. There was nothing left of our lives but the rubble of broken chains under our feet. We all were like newborn babies again – learning to walk and talk in this our new reality. But where do we go? We were free but we were not safe, like lost little children we wandered by the hundreds.

How did we find each other? I dreamt of stardust and roses even if there was only mud on my feet.

I breathed in deeply the unfamiliar smell of freedom and exhaled tears for those who didn't make it.

How did we find each other? We believed that this was our time and place in the world, but they reminded us that it wasn't. You were still called "boy" when you were truly the only man in the room. We cleaned their house and tended to their children, still begging to learn to read.

How did we find each other? Was it the sounds of the Mandinka warriors that lived deep within our souls? Was it the sway in my step like the ocean on the beaches of Nigeria? Or was it the darkness of our skin deep and mysterious like the jungles of the Congo?

How did we find each other? Fate spit at us in the face – but this time when I wiped my eyes you were there. You were always there, my hearts dream spoken to the universe. You were always there, protecting me in the night and fathering children not your own.

You were always there loving me like a Queen when we lived like paupers. You were always there carrying me when I thought I could not walk on. You were always there, and I will always be alongside you.

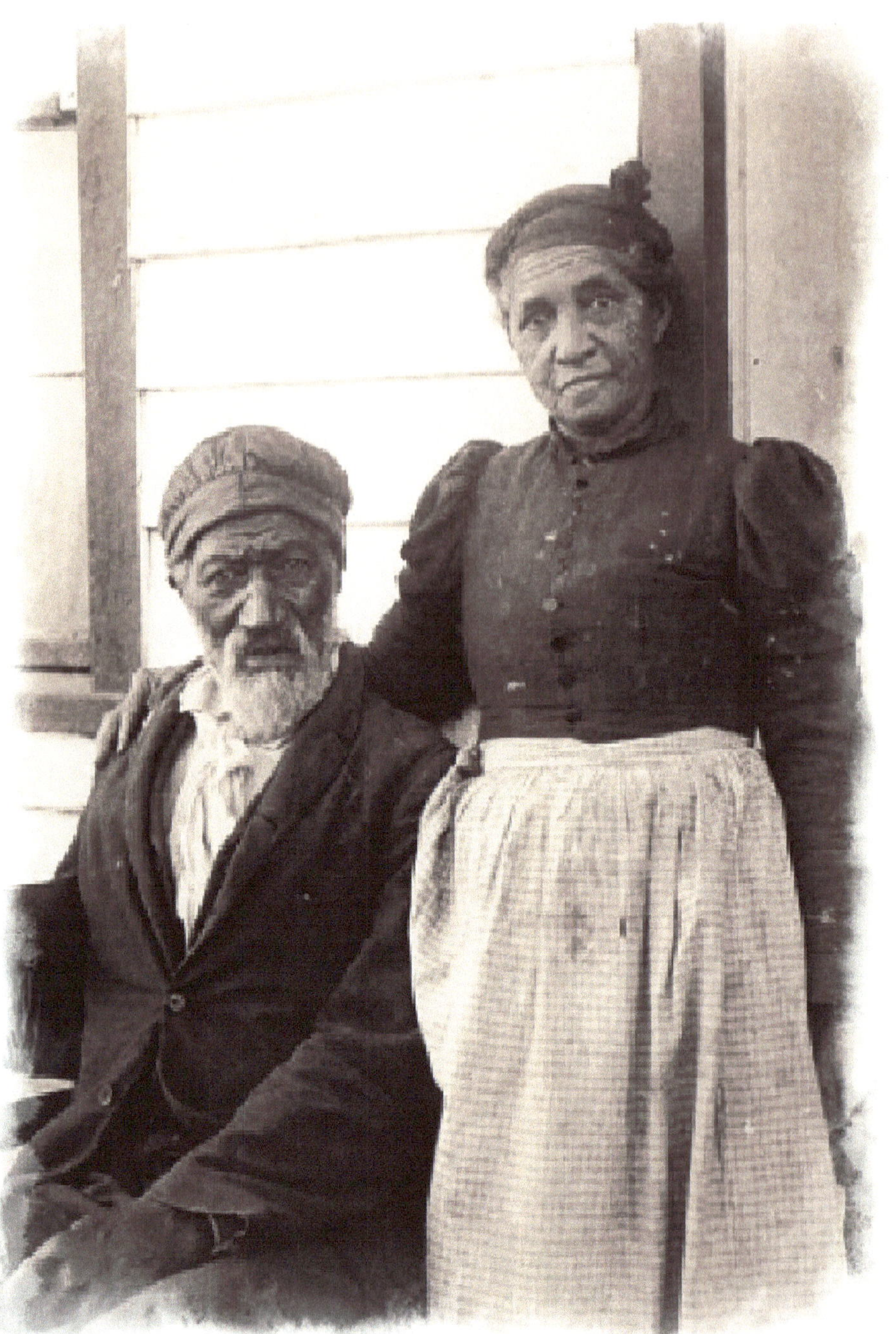

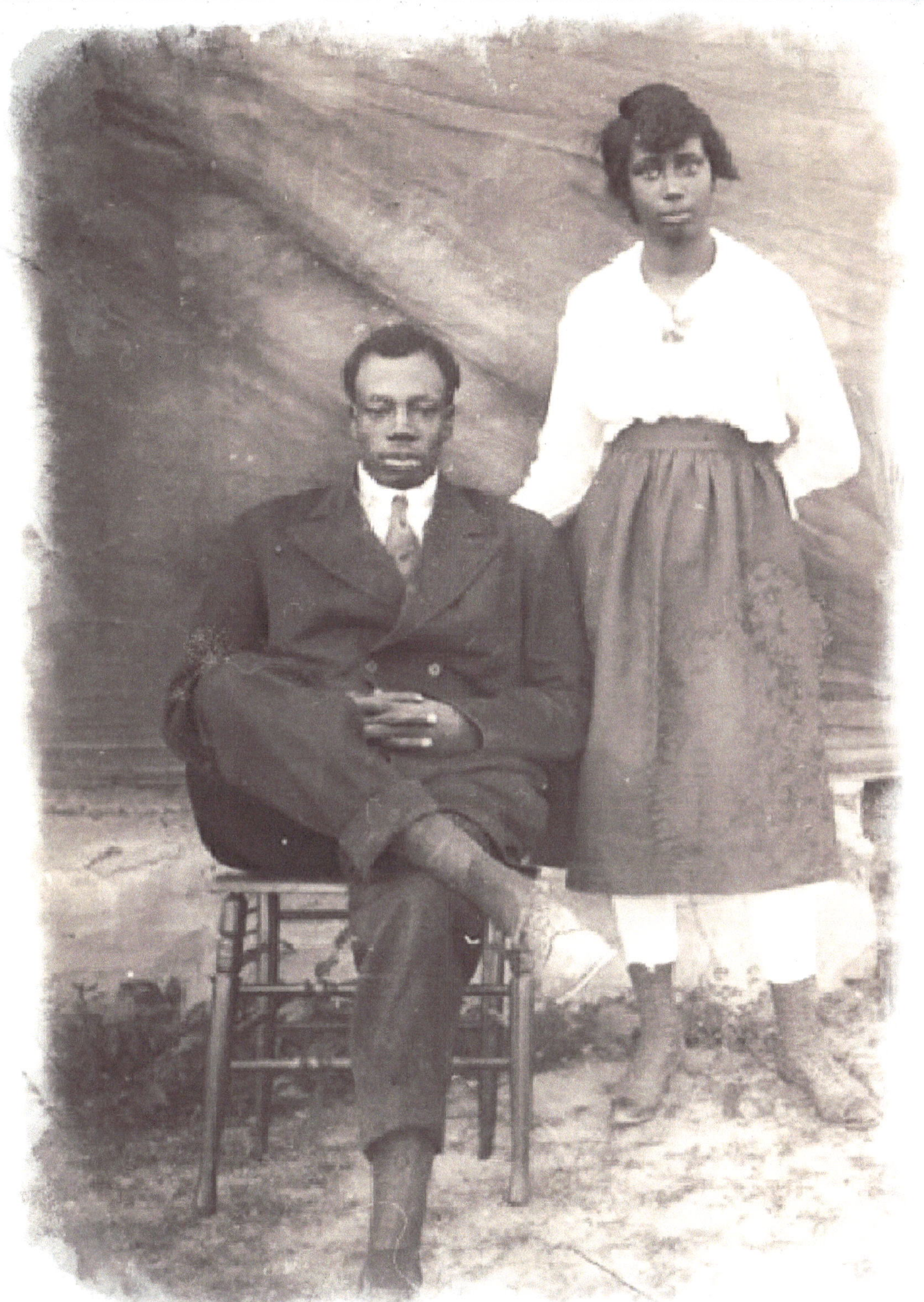

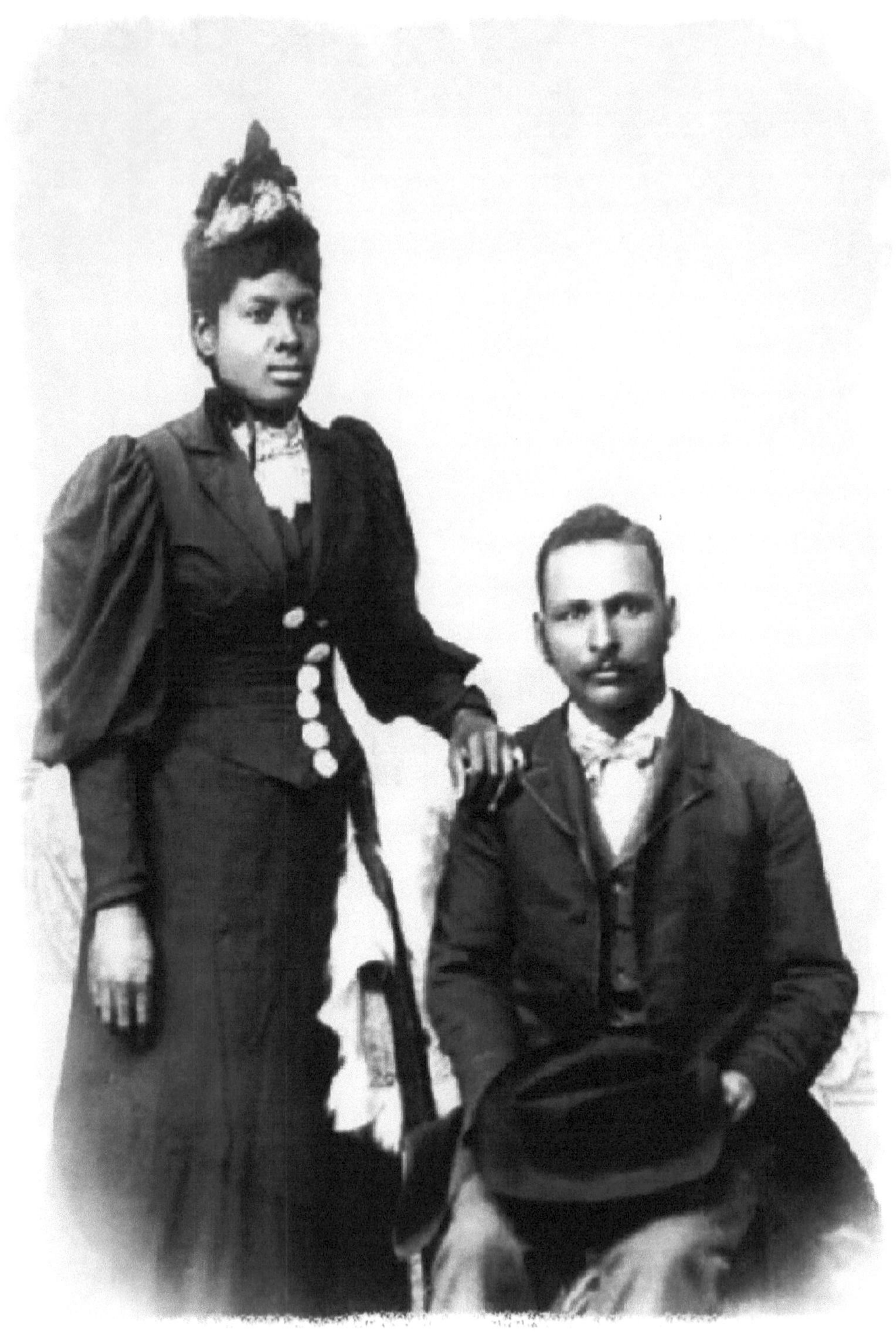

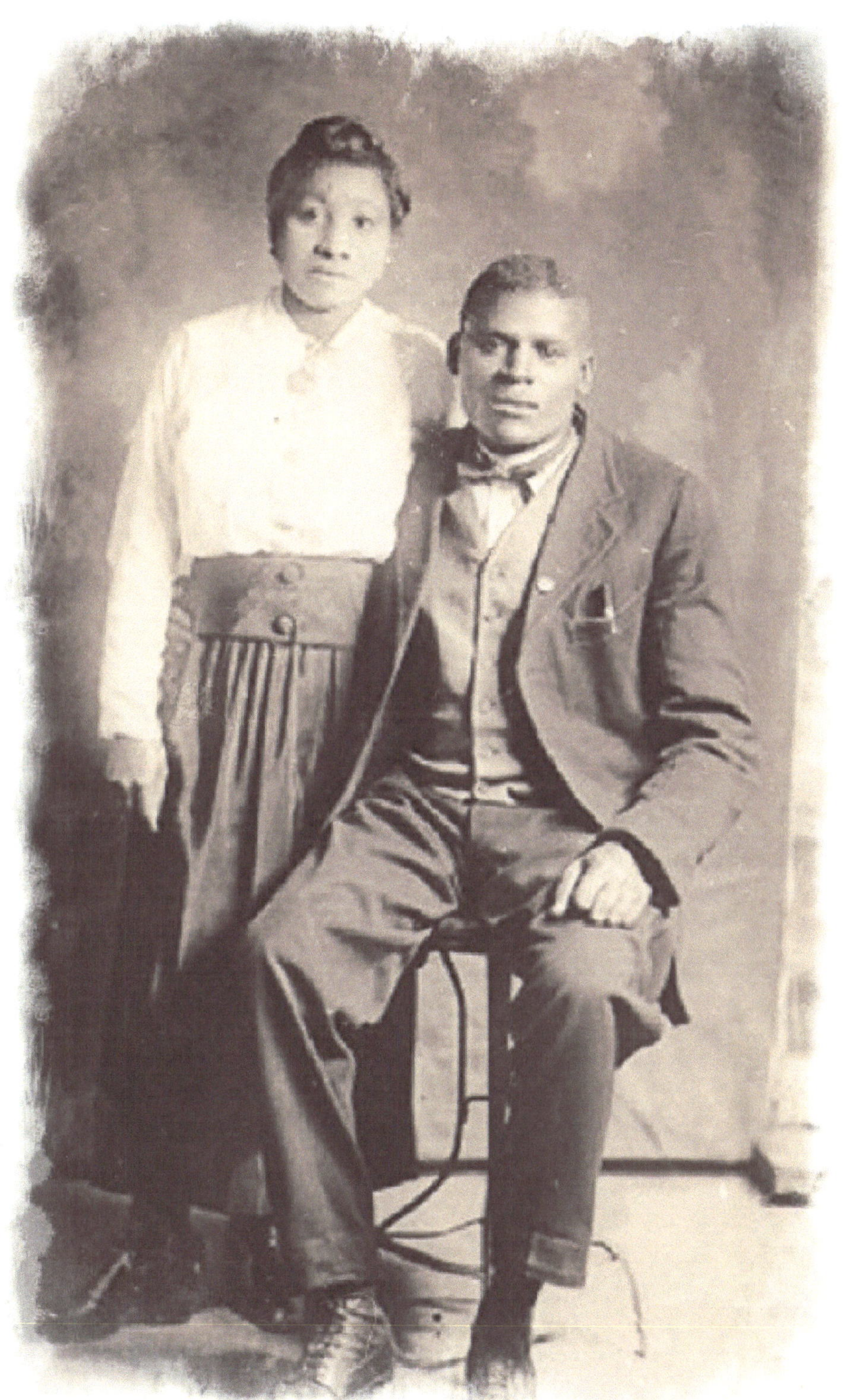

Sweeter than Sweet

He was sweeter than sweet, and his touch like crushed velvet against my skin. I crave him like the finest chocolate I could never get enough. Maybe it was the sound of his voice and the images it painted in my head, or maybe because he embodied the phrase, tall, dark man. I wanted him, I needed him, but not for the seduction of my flesh, but because his words fed my soul.

He said everything and nothing and it spoke to me. He was the gentleman with a passionate beast that lay deep within his chest, and I wanted to discover it and discover every piece and part of him. His quiet seduction of carefully chosen words and grammatically correct sentences licked and tasted my mind, he sent erotic waves of thought through my being.

His intelligence invited me into his world, and I didn't want to leave. I needed his conversation like a junkie needs that fix. I had become addicted and I refused to get clean. I felt a connection at the core of my brain –he expanded my darkened universe and revived the poetry within me.

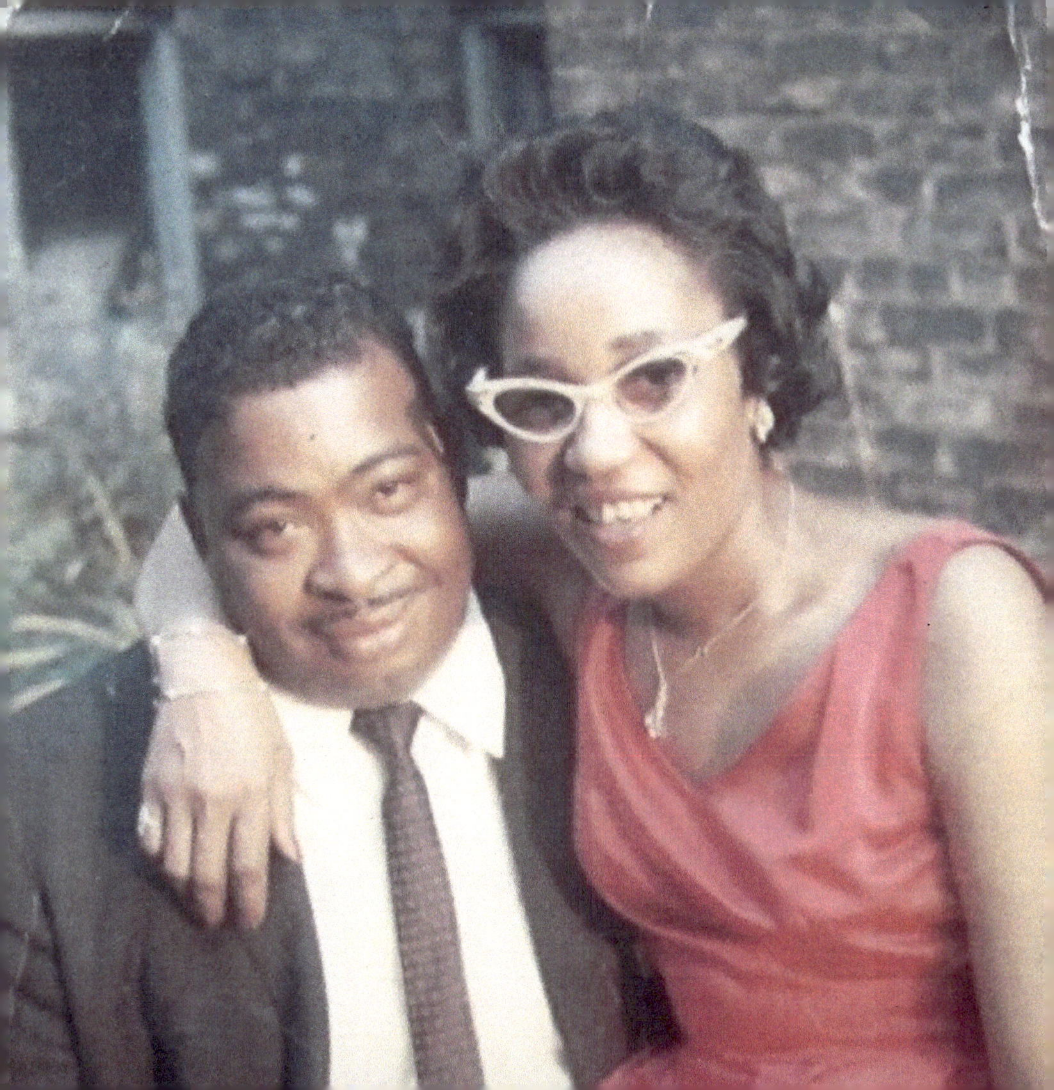

Reverence

You seduced me with one sentence and the falling rain and moonlight became the backdrop of our passion. We were taken hostage by our own impulsive desires and had no care to be free again.

Your power pulled me in like the moon moves the ocean. Your darkness and heat became an insatiable craving, and I awoke after each encounter wanting more.

It was the fullness of your lips, energy of your being, and the blackness of a people that stretches back before recorded time. I touched your scars, and you felt my pain and I could do nothing less than give myself in reverence.

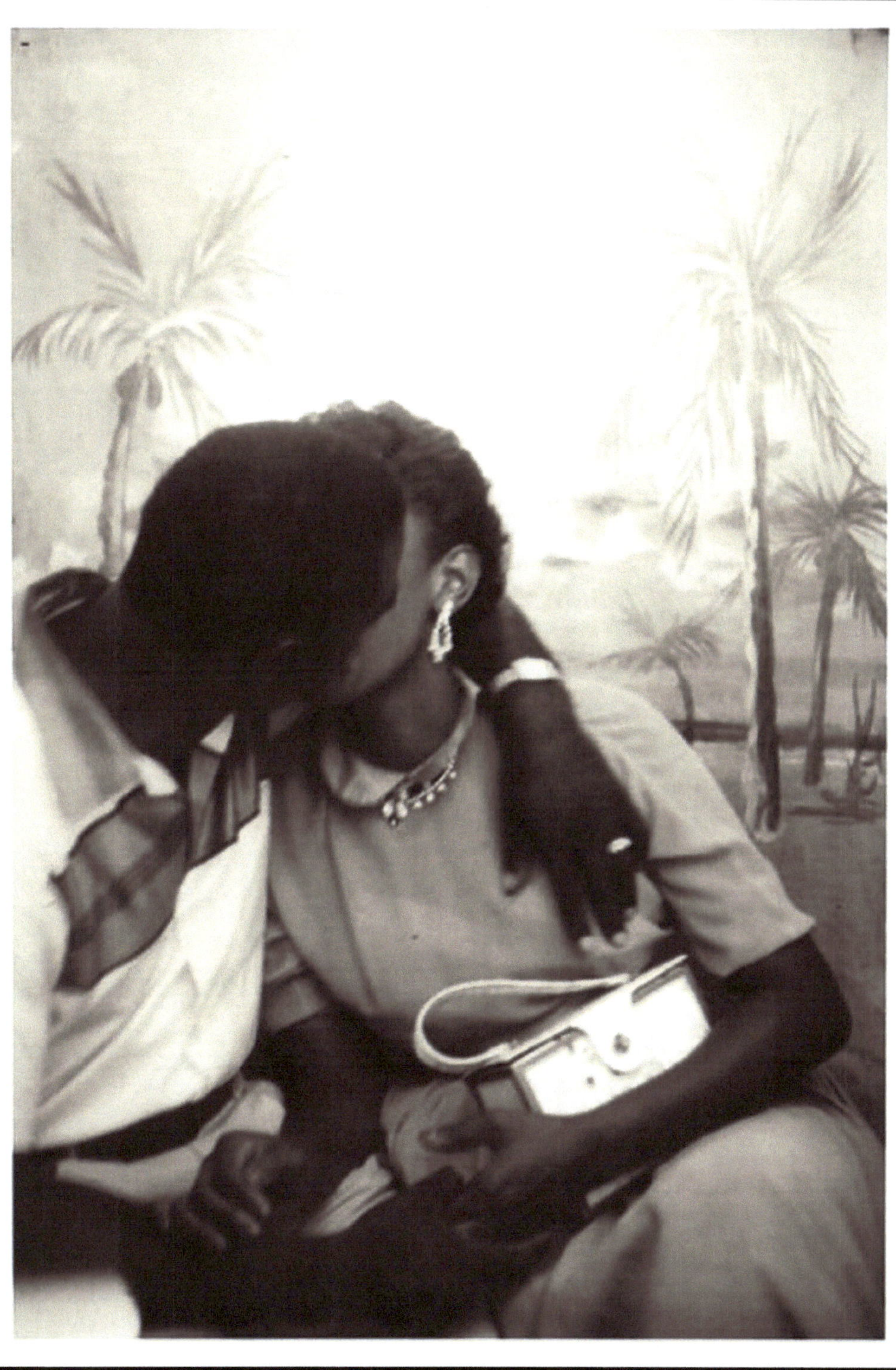

Essence

Your essence reached out to me from across the universal expanse and I felt you through another's touch. What should have been joy and ecstasy became madness and melancholy. I desperately tried not to compare, but how can I not when I have experienced all that passion is within your arms.

Our story ended far too quickly, and you took with you to the heavens my soul, leaving me with this gaping chest wound.

I sank into the abyss of your absence wanting to be loved again, possessed again, needed again. Wondering if a love like yours will ever find its way back into my existence. I am given the words "move-on" like it's the cure for my unending addiction to you, but when you have bonded flesh together it is far too painful to be ripped apart.

Instead, I need compassion and consumption. To feel your lips against my neck and the delight of your fingertips against my spine. I need you in every dimension - to free me from my prison of everyday existence. I need your carnal art form of strength and power to revive me, for there is no home for old lovers... In losing myself I found you, now that you are gone how do I find me again?

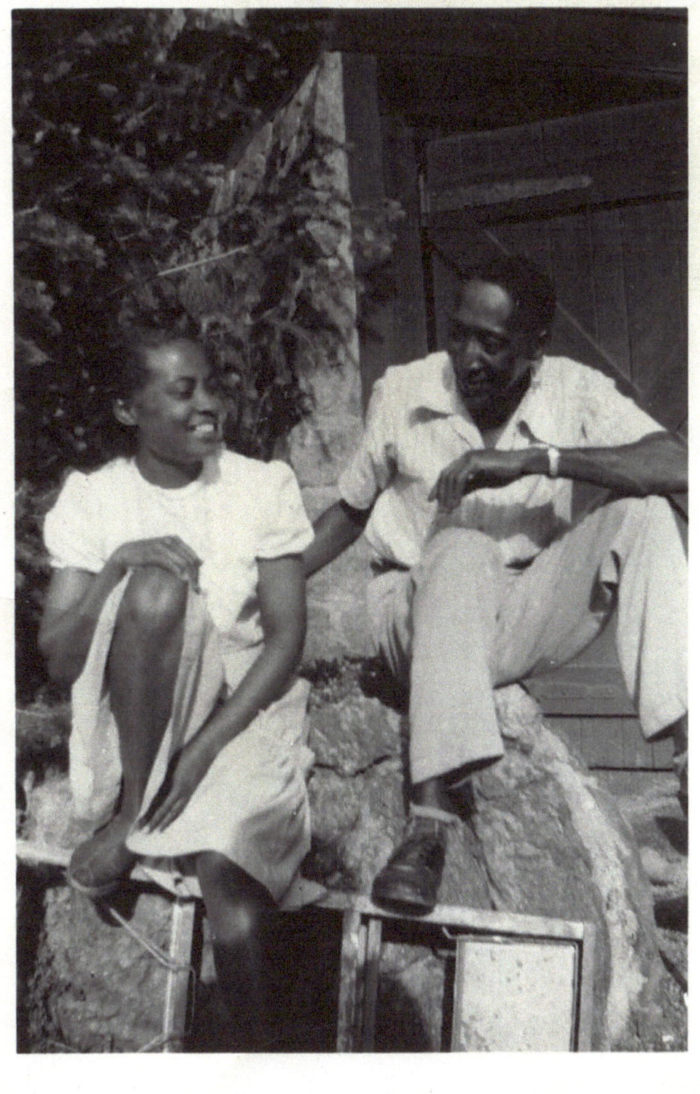

To Be

I am a writer rather than a speaker. I am a believer in all things possible even if I don't see it for myself. I enjoy loving just for the sake of loving. My definition of pleasure is tangled and obscure, but my greatest joy is derived from a sense of security. When I am not secure my habits and goals waiver. When confidence begins to wane, I feel lost and unimportant.

Admittedly I am uniquely complicated, but my heart and dedication outweigh my chaos. To understand me requires only simplistic thoughts and often the understanding never arrives amid the confusion and complexities of other human beings. My personal truth is rooted in childhood pain and adulthood confusion. It is "Sefa" that I long to be daily – an unconventional pleasure that caters to your mental and physical sexuality.

As I lay myself at your feet and leave my mind wide open for your inspection, I am tensed with excitement. My flesh tingles at the very thought of your possession and I thirst and hunger to be your satisfaction.

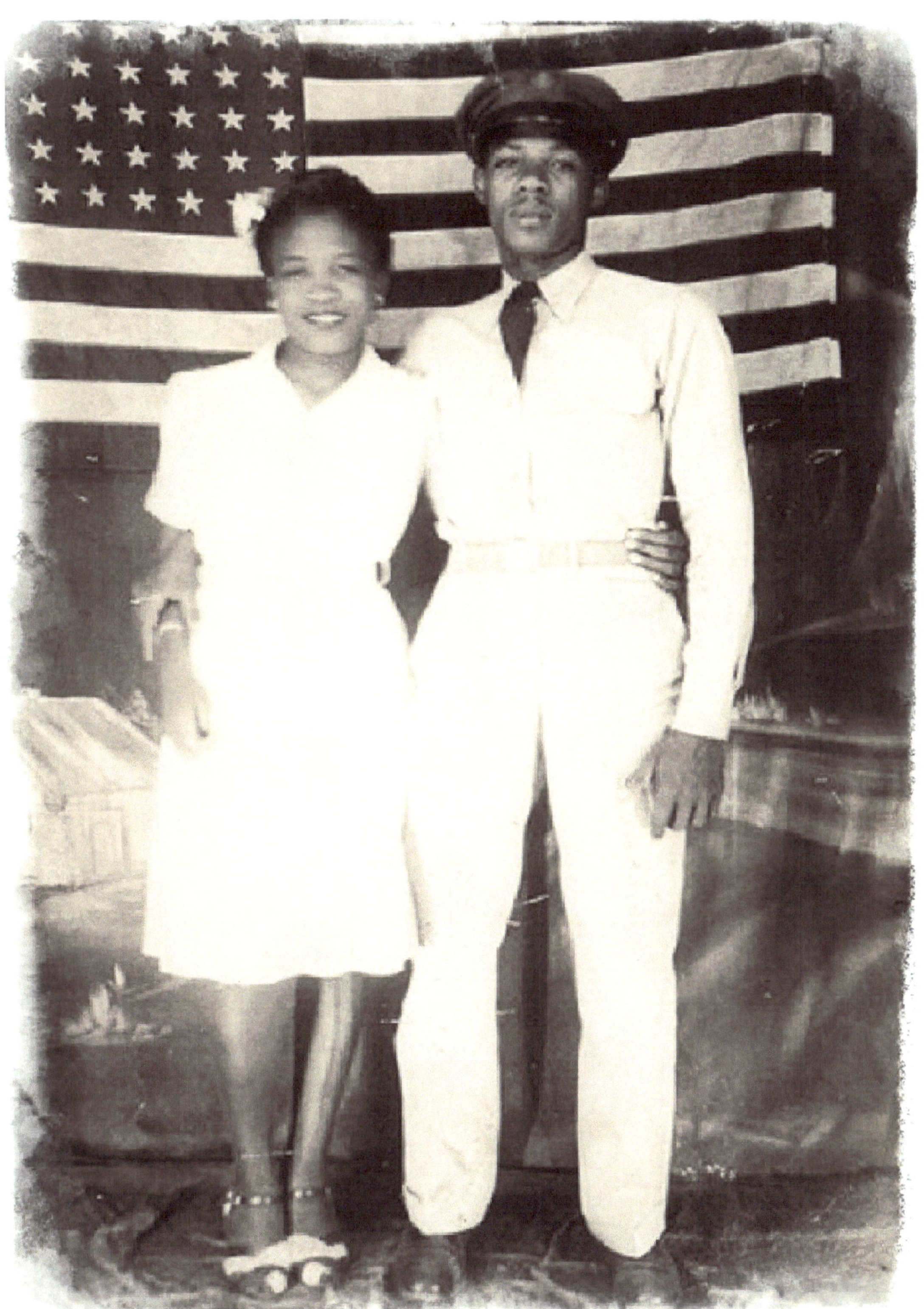

Damisi

I can't promise you forever, but I can give you today, and should the sunrise tomorrow over us I will give you that too. Dreams of rainbows, flowers, and sunshine don't live in our world, but passion and love does. You found me hiding within side myself and you dared me to show you myself, and my truth, and I hated you for it.

Then when I was ready to leave and go back into hiding- You shouted "I love You "at me, and in that instant, you had given me something I had never had – someone who gave a damn. Unlike the meaning of my name, I am not "cheerful" but I am determined.

After that day, I knew that I would do whatever it takes for you to remain in my life. Yet somehow, I felt inside that I was holding you back from your greatness. I needed you – and I needed you more than I was willing to admit, because life had already taught me the hard lesson of not relying on anyone.

People looked at us and wondered what it was that you saw in me. Little did they know the question was what did I see in you that I allowed you in my life, my mind, my heart, and my soul.

You wanted me to believe that I could be better than I am- but I had given up that dream long ago. The goal simply had become to survive – and again you shouted, "I love you" at me and I was forced to believe that happiness existed. Three simple words and you did what prison couldn't do – you broke me.

All I had ever known was fighting – and now I was fighting not to fall in love with you. It became the fight of my life, the battle I could never win. You defeated me, you defeated me and all my senseless pride – but where did that leave us?

Your love and faith in me has never wavered, even when my pockets were empty. How did I find someone like you? How did you find someone like me? I'm going to believe it was my mother in heaven who sent you, because she was tired of seeing me suffer. She promised that last day she'd always be with me – and now I believe in angels.

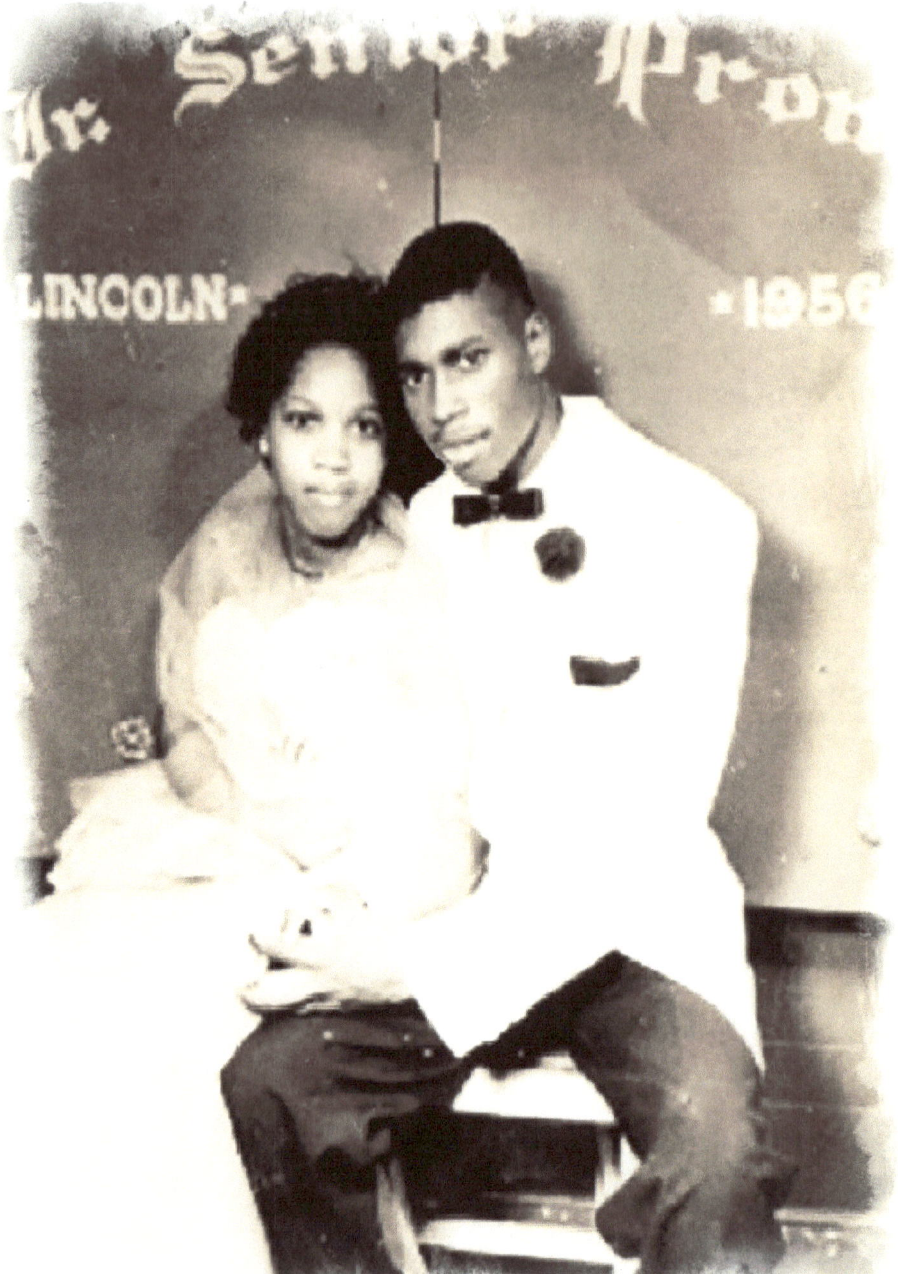
LINCOLN
1956

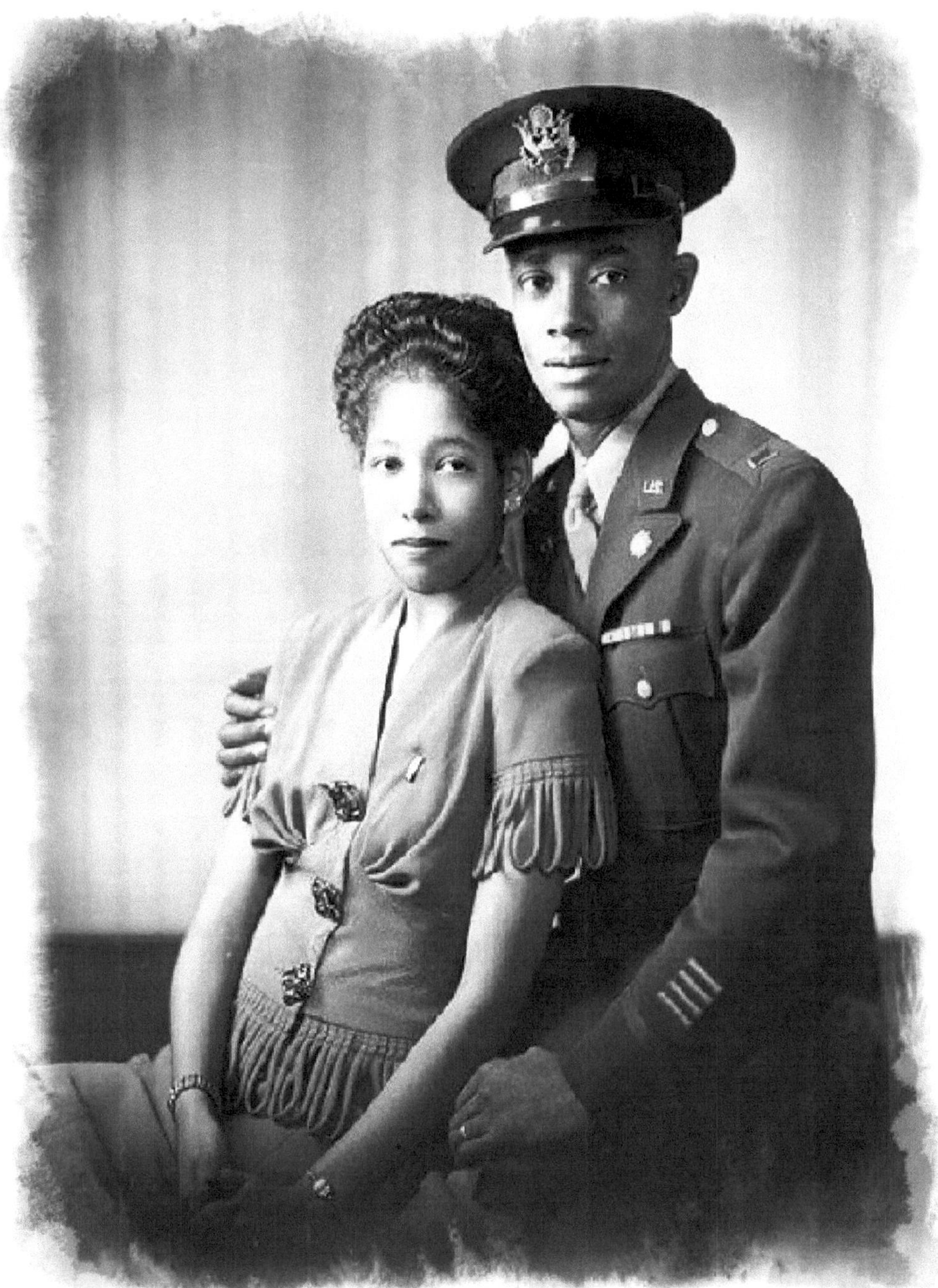

In Love

Lost amid the hazy fog of too many yesterdays and promises of unending tomorrows. I was praised for my strength as I carried on without you and chastised for my anger as my heart is hardened by your absence.

Do you not recognize the cold indignation in my spirit – borne out of loneliness and unending days waiting on your return.

Yes, I am self-sufficient, self-actualized, and self-promoting - but that is just a polite description for my hatred of those who stand in the way of our greatness. We are designed for each other – perfectly by the universe, the jewel in each other's crown. You are Sun and without you, this Earth cannot flourish. We are a balanced scale when joined together, absent from one another we became prey.

You bring life to my future and I hold the stability of your past. An incarnate creation of entities drifting amid someone else's reality.

We took an oath to never be the same, a promise of love at the altar of convention. Wherever you are, I shall follow, love me, and lead me into our tomorrow and show me the beauty of a black woman in love with a black man.

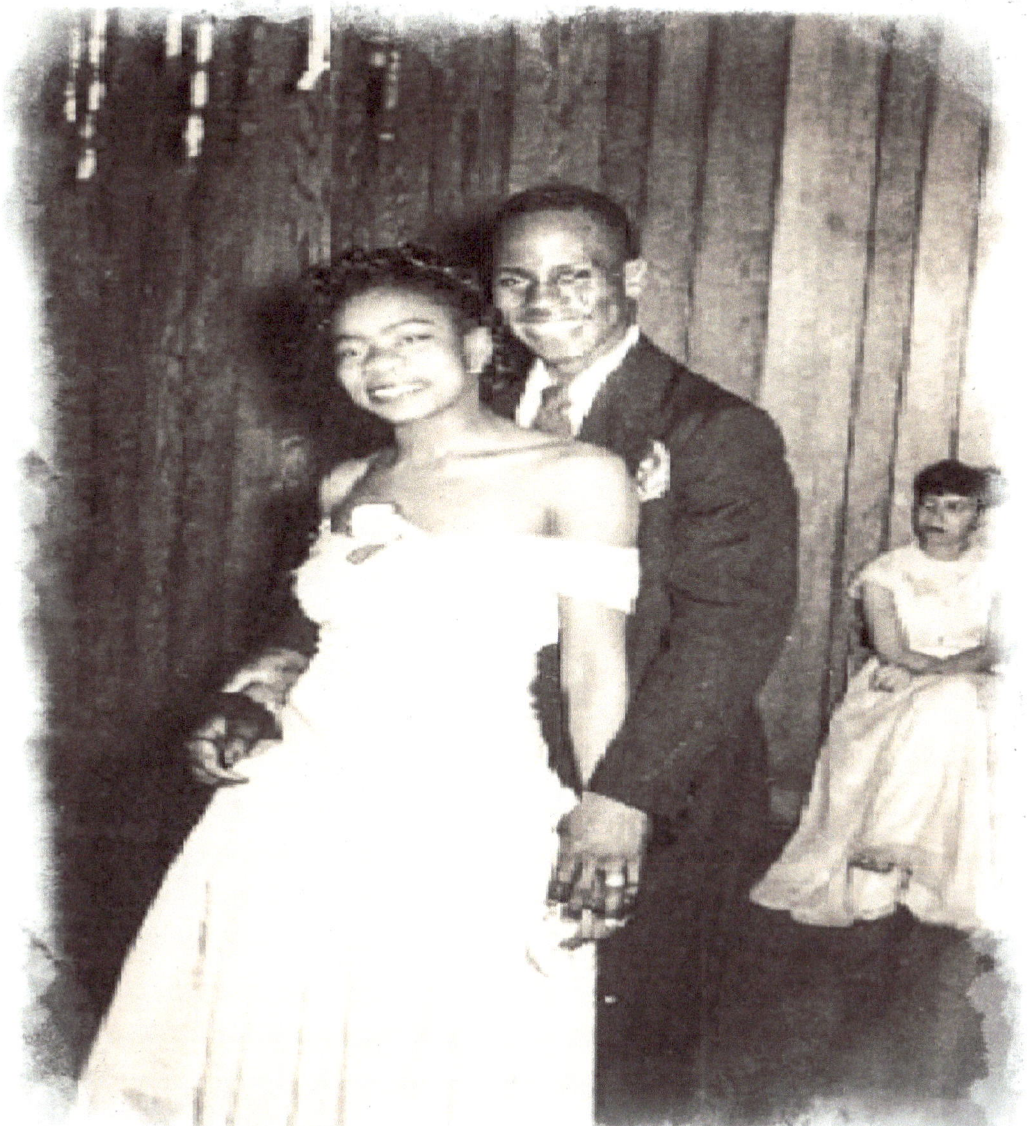

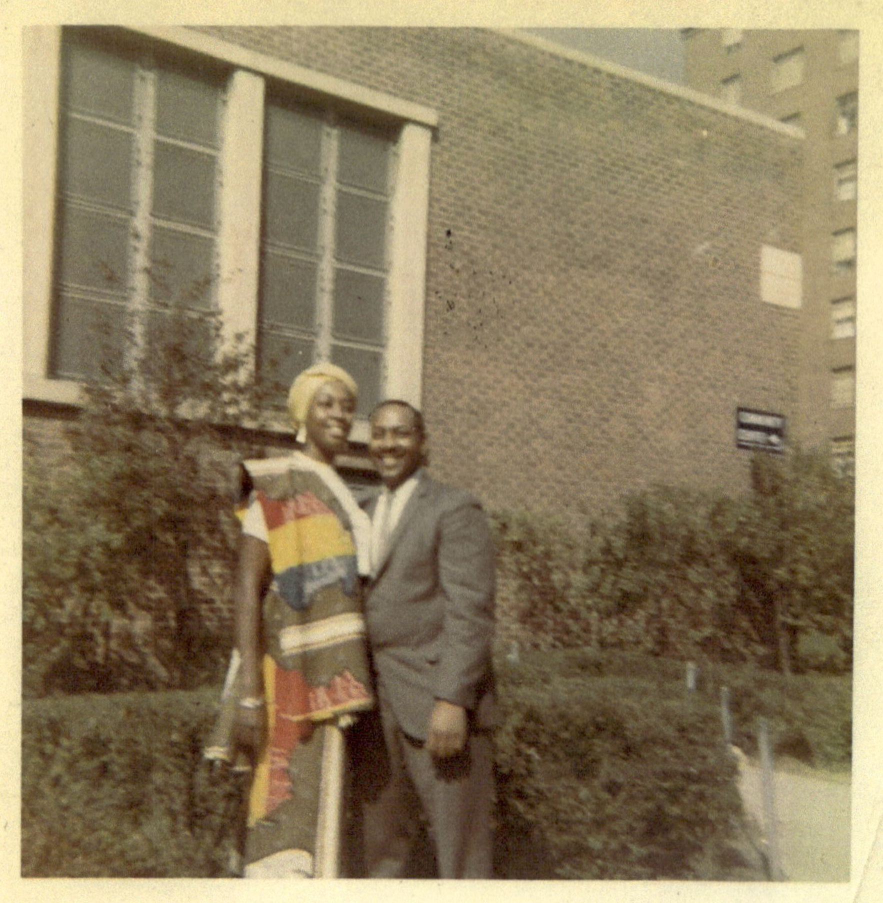

No Other

Words are sacred, in them are the mysteries of life. I seek the meanings in every word from your lips, deep and lush valleys of your thoughts full of the eternally blossoming flowers of each idea.

There is that profound emotional and spiritual connection between us – and sometimes it frightens me.

It frightens me because perfection often comes at the price of pain and much sacrifice. All the suffering of each day longing to be with one another, because there is no other you and I.

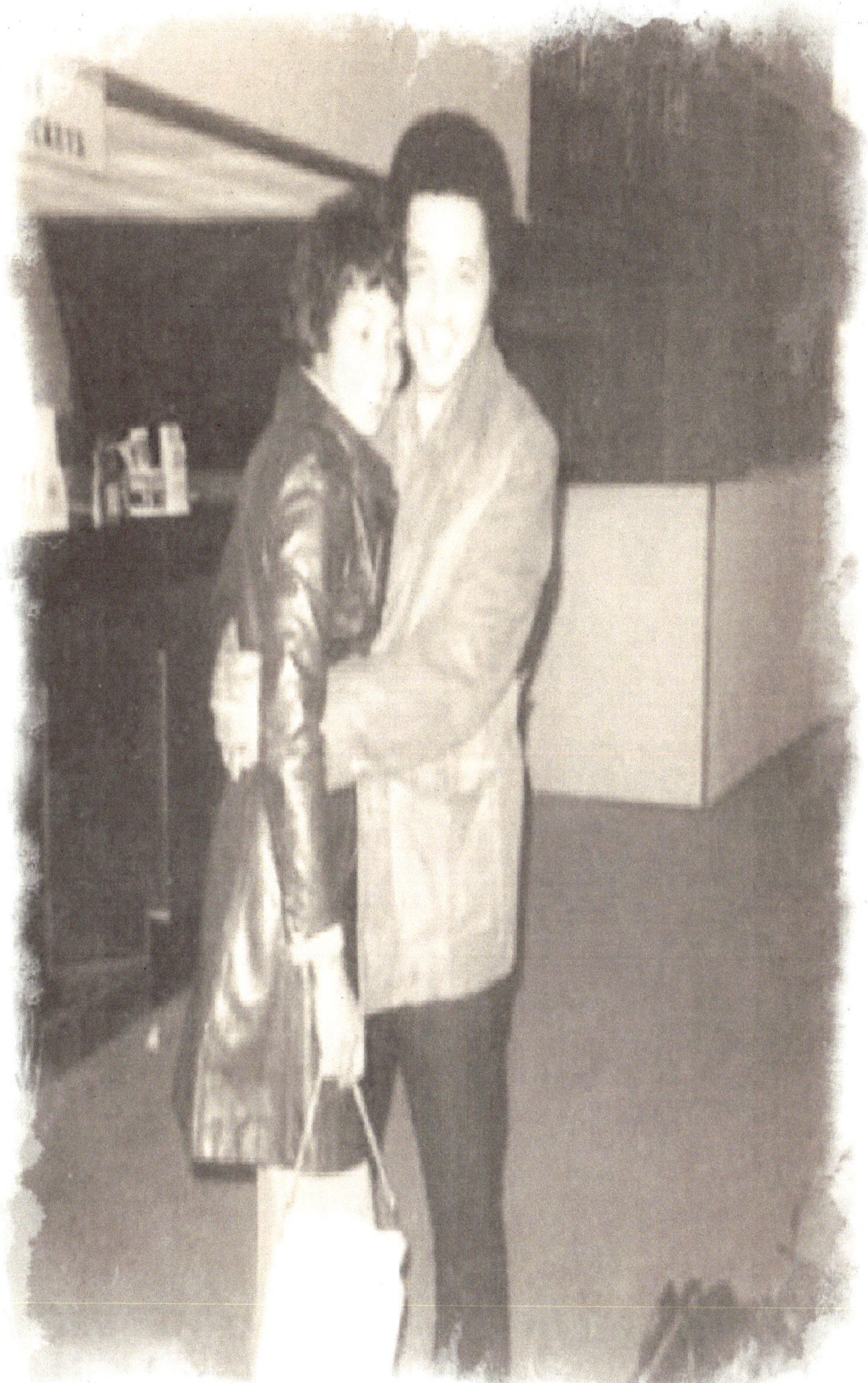

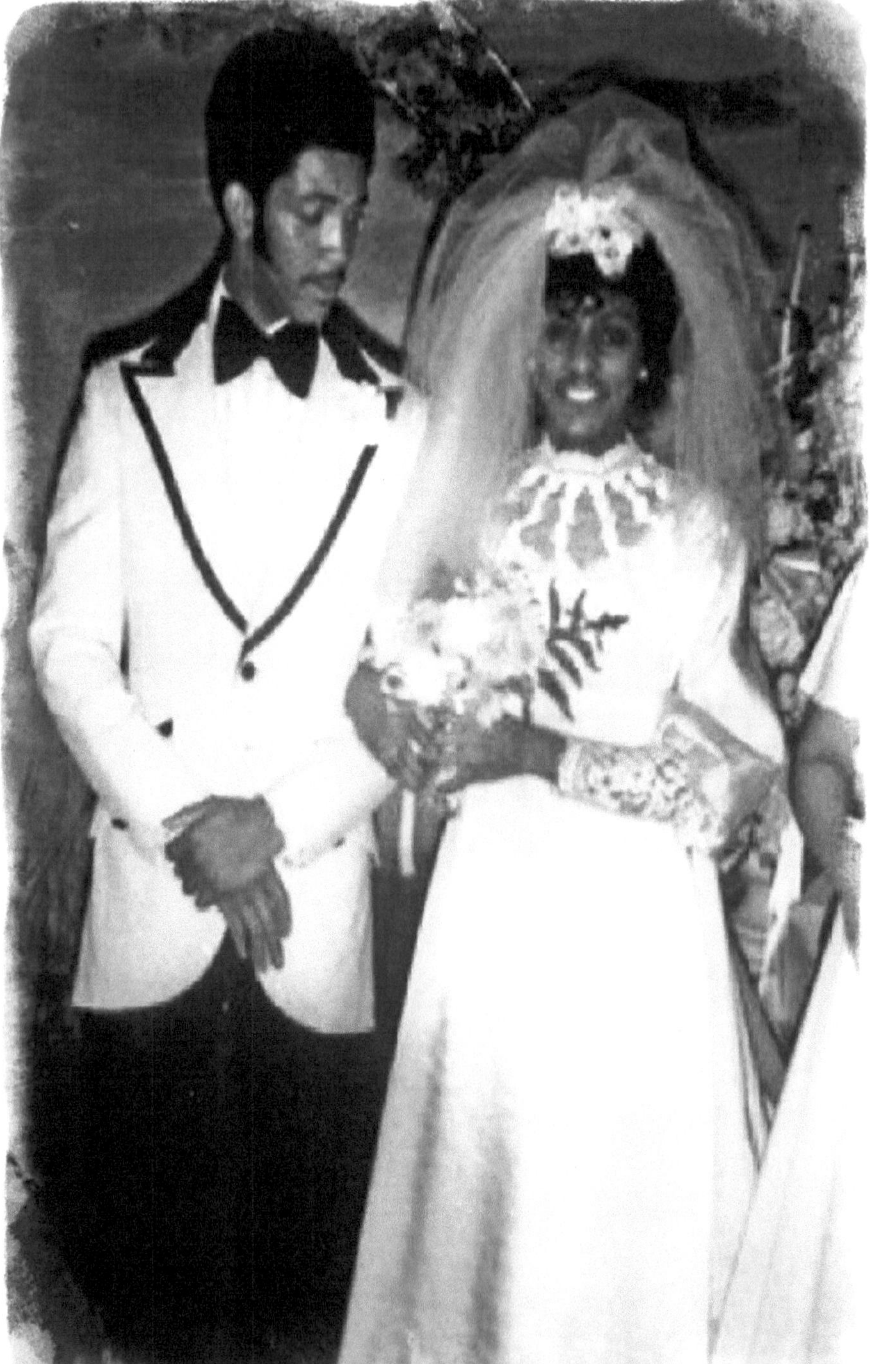

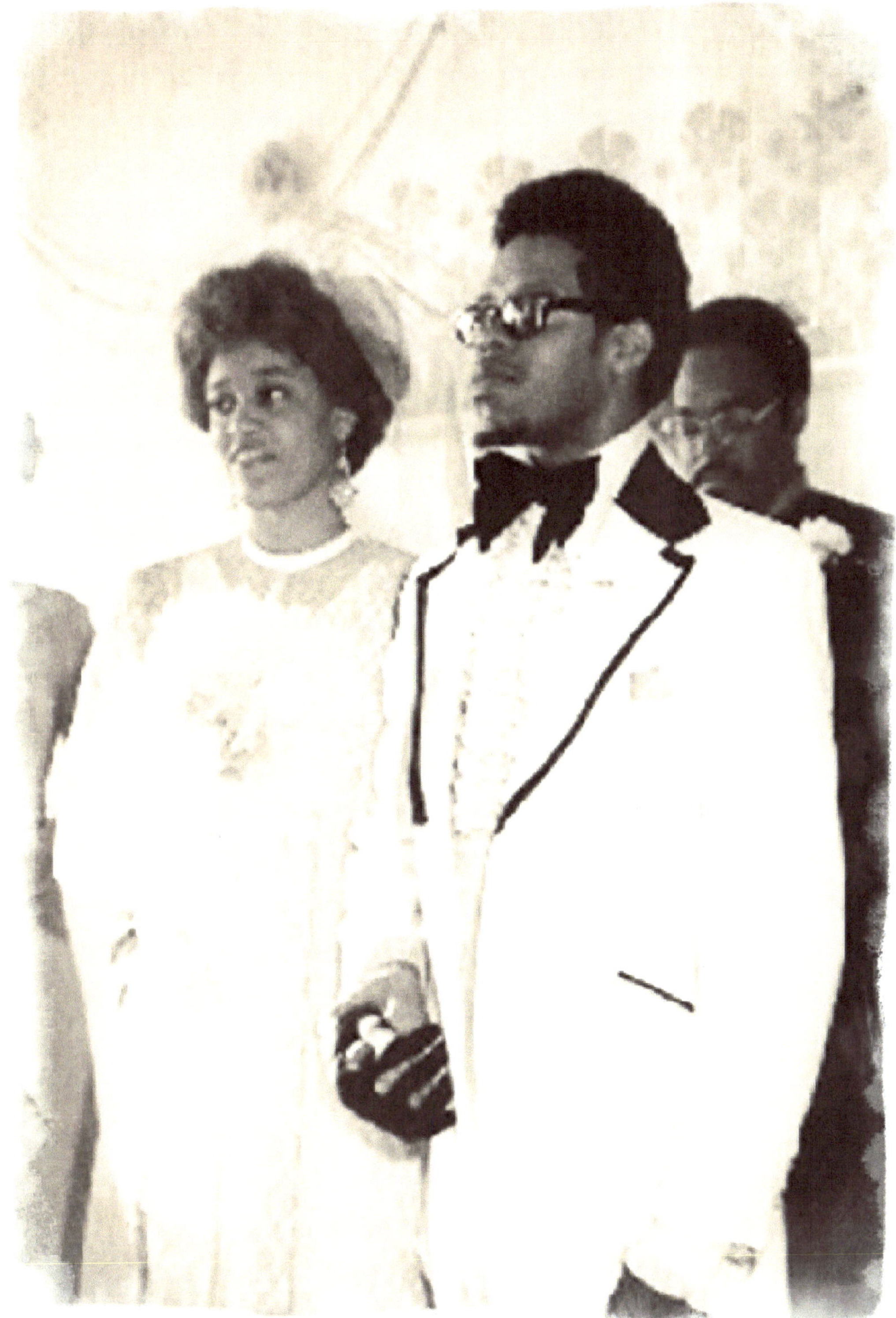

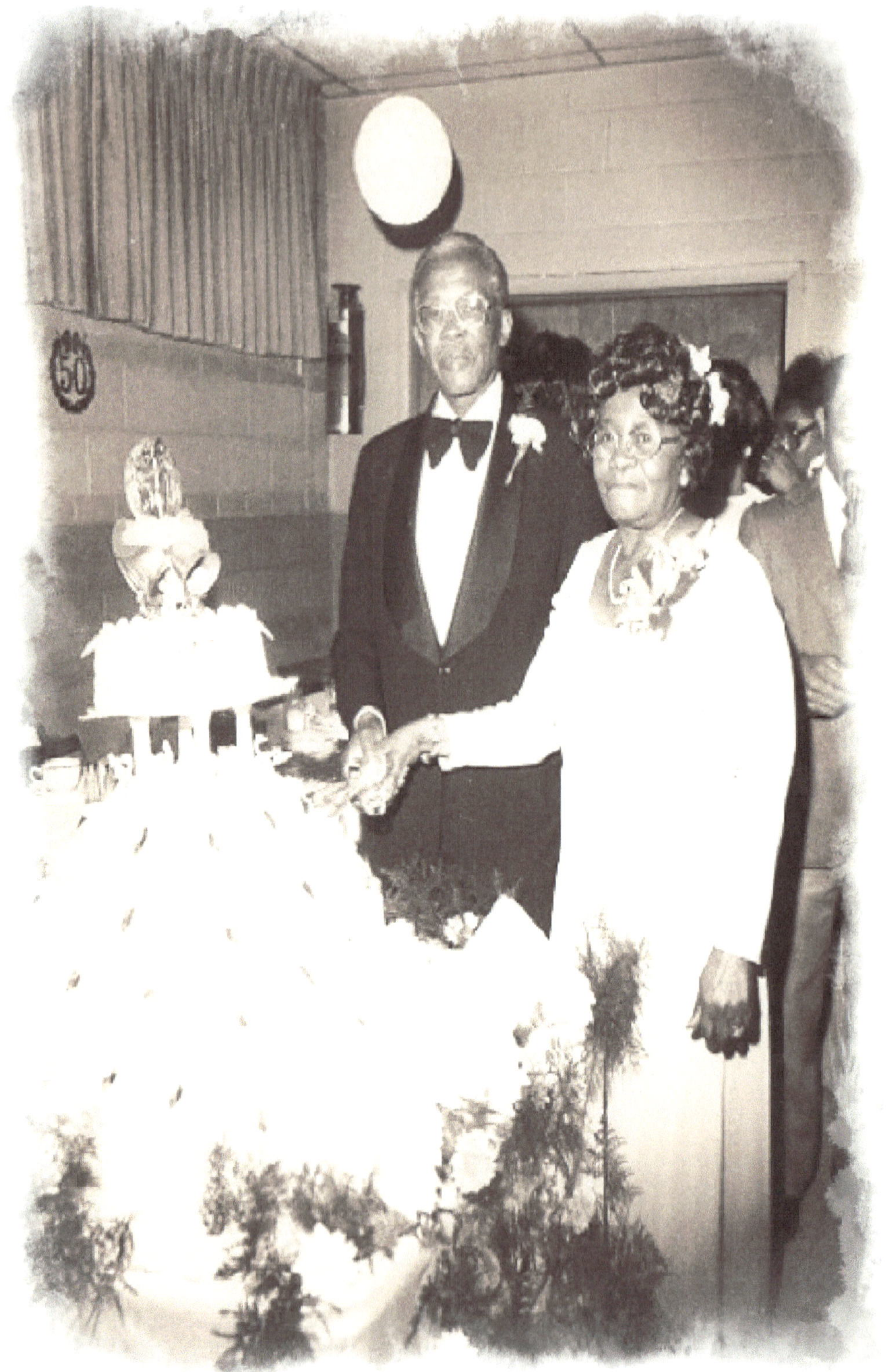
50

COMING SOON

Vintage Black
2
By

SEFA NOIR

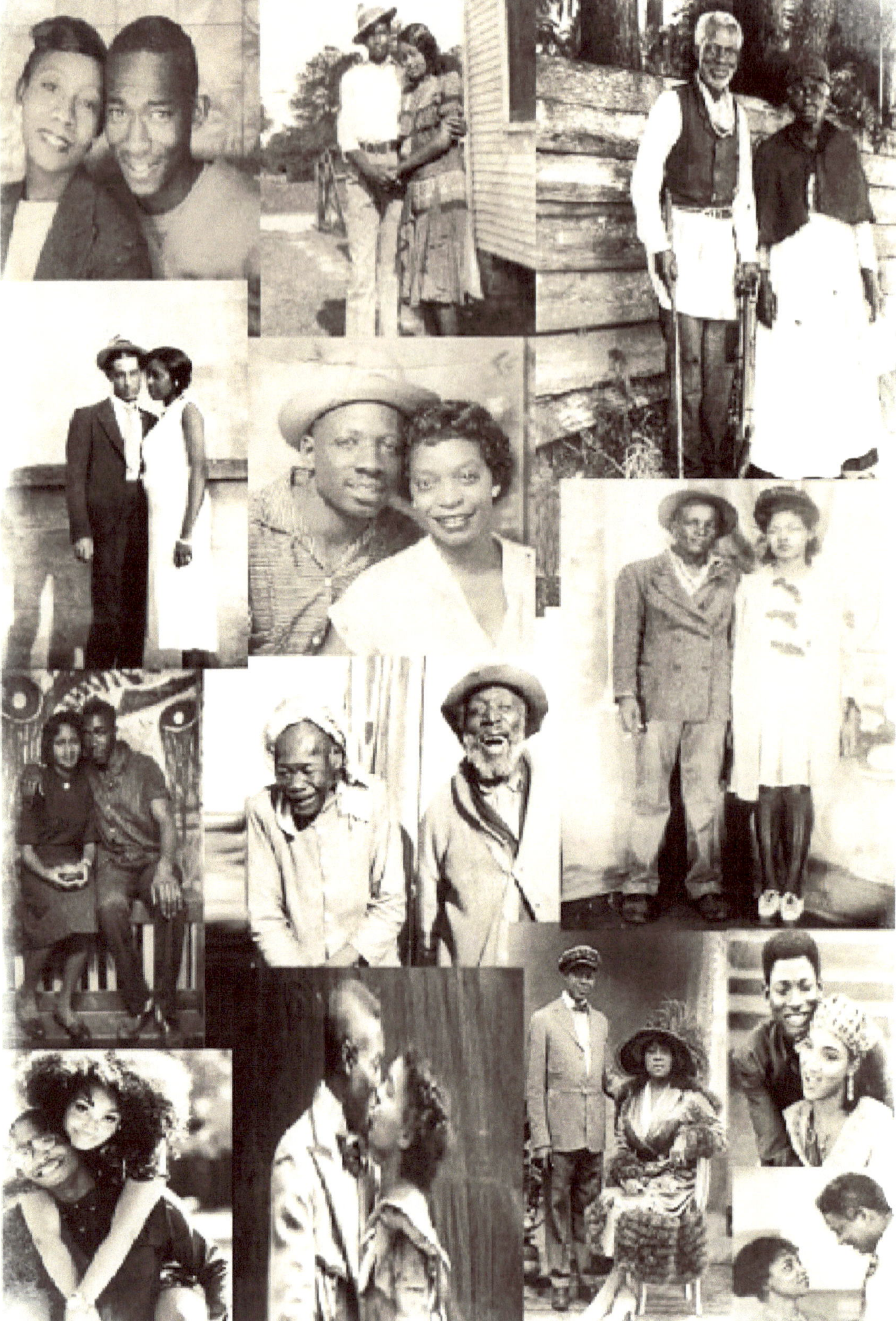

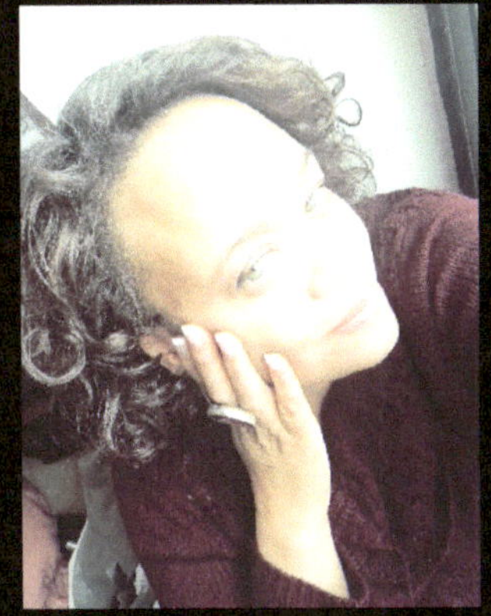

About The Author

Sefa Noir's corporate life is a focused executive HR professional, who mentors' employees on careers and their dreams. When not working as an executive, she writes poetry to record her thoughts, feelings, beliefs and dreams about the human condition, relationships, and love.

Raised in the suburbs of Northern New Jersey, Sefa Noir did all the "right" things and followed every societal rule. Moving through life doing the expected, college, career and family, however underneath her responsibilities beat the heart of a passionate poet and a student of black culture and eroticism.

A self-described submissive female in the Dominant/Submissive sub-culture, Sefa Noir has long been a witness and participant in the beauty of strong black love.

To learn more about Sefa Noir and her upcoming soulful works of poetry, visit her profile on the publishing website:

www.AJBPublishing.com or follow her on Instagram @Sefa_Noir

www.ingramcontent.com/pod-product-compliance
Lightning Source LLC
LaVergne TN
LVHW070157110826
845147LV00002B/430
* 9 7 8 0 5 7 8 8 6 8 0 3 5 *